Wheels Around Perth

by
Alan Brotchie

A busy South Street scene looking west to County Place with York Place in the distance. There is much pedestrian traffic but the street is surprisingly empty of vehicles. A lone cyclist passes a horse-drawn coal delivery cart. The old two- and three-storey buildings on the left have been replaced, but the arched windows of the former meeting hall to the right are still to be seen.

THE PUBLISHERS REGRET THAT THEY CANNOT SUPPLY
COPIES OF ANY PICTURES FEATURED IN THIS BOOK.

ACKNOWLEDGEMENTS

I wish to acknowledge the help freely given and gratefully received from
A. Condie, R. L. Grieves, J. J. Herd and the staff of the A. K. Bell Library.

Guddling at the pond at Buckie Braes, to the south of Cherrybank; note the garden barrow of the lad in the foreground. A tram ride to the nearby terminus often formed the starting point for a walk through the quiet woods here – a pleasant memory for many courting couples. On the right is Cock Robin's Well. In the background stand reminders of the First World War – two field guns donated to the city in poignant remembrance of the many local young men who did not return. This area was purchased by the city in 1914, just prior to the outbreak of war. To encourage use of the trams to Cherrybank, the Tramways Department used to hire the Fechney School Band to give recitals, both here at Buckie Braes and at Scone. In one week receipts rose by £63 – a lot of 1*d*. and 2*d*. fares!

INTRODUCTION

As a geographical route focus it is unlikely that Perth has any equal in Scotland. Its position at the lowest bridging point across the River Tay ensured that it would always act as a node point for transport, even from the earliest days. The Romans may have built the first bridge – it has been stated in an old gazetteer that Agricola built a timber bridge towards the end of the first century AD. A successor in stone was swept away in October 1210, and its replacement – a short-lived affair of wood and stone – succumbed to the river's force in 1621. The site of the supposed Roman bridge is not known, but medieval bridges were on the line of the High Street. For the next 150 years a ferry was in use until, on a site some distance further upstream, the still existing nine-arch red sandstone structure was built, designed by John Smeaton. Only 22 feet in width originally, it was widened in 1869 with new footpaths on iron brackets. In this form it has successfully withstood all attempts by the Tay in spate to remove it! The floods of January 1993 inundated large areas and caused considerable damage, although the depths of flood incised on the north-west abutment of the 'dry' arch leading to the North Inch show that even this level was exceeded by some eighteen inches in 1814. However, the city should never be threatened again, with a major permanent flood prevention scheme now (summer 2001) approaching completion.

While the river created the logic for the position of Perth, it was the arrival of the railway which ensured the city's rapid nineteenth century expansion. The first railway to reach the Fair City – as Perth is universally known – was along the Carse from Dundee in May 1847 (although it only reached as far as Barnhill at that time).

The Scottish Central Railway route from Stirling arrived in May 1849, with the Scottish Midland Junction line reaching northwards to Forfar in August of the same year. Perth's location at the hub of a true spider's web of routes was confirmed by the opening of further lines, namely the Edinburgh and Northern route to Burntisland and the trunk line to Inverness in 1863. These reinforced Perth's crucial role as an interchange centre.

Local investors were caught up in the great railway financial crash of 1847. In his privately printed *Reminiscences of my Life in the Highlands*, Joseph Mitchell refers to 'the vortex of railway speculation which was rife throughout the country, particularly in Perth, and by which about half the well-to-do people in that city were damaged and many ruined'. But the railways were built and ultimately employed over 2,000 local men – making a major contribution to the city's economy.

Perth survived the swingeing Beeching cuts with one exception. The last main line to be constructed, the NBR's Glenfarg connection to the Forth Railway Bridge, opened 1890, and was the first main line to close in January 1970. Today the station still boasts many regular departures to Inverness, Aberdeen, Glasgow, Edinburgh and Dundee.

Still a route focus in the twenty-first century, Perth lies at the hub of radiating trunk roads and motorways to all points of the compass. The local scene changed drastically for the better when much through traffic was intercepted by the Friarton bridge – opened in 1978 to the east – and the bypass road to the west, which combined to relieve congestion, particularly on South Street. It is difficult to consider now how the phenomenal recent growth in road traffic could possibly have been catered for in the city centre, without the benefits following from these major road improvements. Since I had the pleasure of living in Perth, and later Scone, many years ago, great change has taken place. I hope this collection brings as many happy memories to the reader as its compilation did to the author.

Right: Lower Scone with horse bus, prior to construction of the horse tramway in 1895. The Scone & Perth Omnibus Co. Ltd. was inaugurated on 1 June 1863 'for carrying of passengers and goods in an omnibus . . . between such places as the Company shall determine'. The initial major shareholders were the Scone Free Church minister and his wife, Revd and Mrs Charles Stewart, the chairman being James Mitchell, draper, also from Scone. The bus became a local institution and was in operation for 21 years. It ran six times a day from Perth Cross, journeying the three miles to the top end of Scone Village and less frequently to Balbeggie.

The Scone & Perth Omnibus Co. was bought over – amicably – by a newly-formed horse tramway company on 8 May 1894, and the former bus company shed in Perth Road, New Scone, was soon equipped as the tram depot. Its three gables can be seen facing the street in this evocative 100-year-old view. The tram stands at the terminus, outside the depot and stables. The road is only water-bound macadam, which was dusty in summer and muddy in winter. On the right the small child is standing at the water well or standpipe; few houses then had the luxury of a mains water supply.

No wheels close to the photographer, but plenty in the distance. Friarton Hill was a popular location for viewing the panorama of Perth, the Tay and the harbour. In this particular picture there is much to note including the newly-constructed raw embankment of the Caledonian Railway harbour branch. Friarton Road is yet to be built to the west side of the harbour. Small salmon-fishing dories are beached on the tidal 'grasslands', and the early nineteenth century bulk of Perth Prison – still in use to this day – overlooks the scene. All the development between the railway and the harbour – dominated by the tall sawmill chimney which also appears newly built – is indicative of the rapid expansion of the town at this time.

A Caledonian Railway goods train making its way down the single-track branch line to the harbour. To the left the track crossed Shore Road where a reversal was necessary to propel the wagons to the harbour – on the return journey the locomotive would push the train back up to the main line junction. With his 'steam' joinery works, Falconer emphasised that elsewhere much timber sawing was still done by hand, using long saws operated by two men, one of whom was positioned in a 'saw pit'. Timber production was one of the surrounding area's major industries. David Douglas of Scone is perhaps the best-known local arboriculturist, his name forever connected with the Douglas Fir imported by him from North America.

Perth's horse trams lingered on – as commemorated by this postcard – until 31 October 1905. By this time the larger Scottish cities had all converted to electric traction. The Perth & District Company had been bought over by the Corporation on 15 May 1903, at a cost of £21,800 (equivalent in purchasing power to about £1 million in 2001). For this sum the Corporation acquired nine horse trams, with very limited shelf-life, 4¼ miles of track which had to be immediately reconstructed, and the Scone tram depot. It is believed that the company shareholders were not unhappy with the deal. Two of the redundant vehicles are seen passing at the High Street/Scott Street crossroads with, on the right, the disproportionate bulk of the old post office building. Dating from 1898, this was demolished in 1974.

IN AFFECTIONATE REMEMBRANCE OF

RING OUT THE OLD RING IN THE NEW

THEY DID THEIR WORK THEIR DAY IS DONE

THE PERTH HORSE CARS
WHICH SUCCUMBED TO AN ELECTRIC SHOCK ON TUESDAY OCTOBER 31ST 1905

As well as the last horse trams, the same photographer (J. K. Thompson) recorded the very first electric ones. The Corporation built its depot for the new electric cars on the same site (at the top end of New Scone) as the building that had been used by the horse buses and horse trams. This picture shows car 1, probably on the first day of operation – 31 October 1905 – judging by the large number of interested spectators. All twelve Corporation cars were similar, although three were three inches lower in the saloon to give extra clearance under the King Street railway bridge. The fare from Scone to Cherrybank was 3½d. a not inconsiderable sum bearing in mind that the hourly wage of an artisan was not much more than 6d. However few people went from terminus to terminus – except perhaps for a Sunday day out. The fare to the Cross was 2d. The bowler-hatted figure to the left is Mr Snell – then traffic superintendent – who was promoted to become tramway manager in February 1912. He held this position until September 1928 when the end of the trams was in sight. The sender of this card recorded 'I have had a fine sail up to Perth today'.

PERTH ROAD NEW SCONE

7

Pleasure sailings on the Tay from Broughty Ferry and Dundee were extremely popular prior to the First World War, and some continued until the 1930s. Here the paddle steamer *Carlyle* sets off well-laden from Newburgh, with Perth upstream to the left. A call was also usually made at Bridge of Earn, and sometimes a circuit of Mugdrum Island was included. The *Carlyle* was one of a group of similar vessels that were built in 1905 for London County Council, which intended to run a service between the City, Greenwich and Gravesend after the run was given up by its previous operator. The LCC soon found that they were unable to make the service profitable either and the fleet was sold off. Two vessels, *Carlyle* and sister ship *Alleyn*, came to the Tay in 1909, the former remaining until 1915 under the command of Captain John Todd. Then requisitioned for war service, she undertook her longest journey, travelling by way of the Cape of Good Hope to the Persian Gulf. She was sunk in the River Tigris in what is now Iraq, during April 1916, while participating in operations for the relief of Kut al Imara (Al Kut).

Scone Market

The new electric trams prompted a flurry of activity from picture postcard printers, all anxious to be totally up to date. Perth trams arrived during the heyday of the picture postcard – it was estimated that in the Edwardian years tens of thousands were sent daily. This was in the era before telephones, and with up to six deliveries per day in some cities, it was possible to send a postcard and receive a reply later the same day. A major blow was dealt to this success story when the postage rate was doubled – from ½d. to one (old) penny! This postcard, featuring obligatory tram, dates from 1906 and shows car no. 2 heading away from the terminus. A small market was held once a week at Cross Street at the foot of Perth Road, and in this picture ice-cream carts seem to predominate. The view has altered remarkably little today, with the Scone Arms still occupying its corner site, although the house with forestair in the foreground on the right has been demolished.

PERTH BRIDGE.

849.

On their route into town the trams passed through Bridgend, then turned through 90 degrees to cross Perth Bridge. Here car 12 is heading west across the bridge to Cherrybank. Until construction of the Victoria Bridge in 1900 this was the lowest road crossing over the river. It was designed by John Smeaton and completed in 1770. There had been earlier bridges over the Tay at Perth but all fell to floods over the centuries. The only major alteration to Smeaton's bridge was the provision, in 1869, of cantilevered iron balustrades in place of his stone parapets. That the 880-foot long bridge still carries – without any weight restriction – traffic of the twenty-first century is a testimony to his design and the work of the stonemasons who built it.

Tay Street, Perth.   209.

The last, western arch of Smeaton's bridge crosses not the River Tay, but the extension of Tay Street leading to the North Inch, an area of almost 100 acres understood to have been granted to the town in 1377 by King Robert II. Carved on the stone pillar on the left are the heights of inundations by the river – the most recent being the devastating flood of 1993. This, however, is not the highest recorded flood and the uppermost mark – some eighteen inches above the 1993 level – is dated 1814. Following the 1993 flood nearly £25 million has been devoted to major civil engineering works in an endeavour to a avoid repetition. These works have yet to be tested by the river to prove their effectiveness. Two lads with bicycles keep a wary eye on the photographer, who was working for the Kirkcaldy publisher, Davidson & Son.

Watching the river go by – always something there to catch the attention. The young lad in the foreground appears to have a pair of wheels from a perambulator. Smeaton's bridge can just be made out on the left with the houses of Bridgend on the far side of the river. The railings are all away now, having been replaced by a sandstone-faced concrete wall – a major feature of the recent flood defence works. The avenue of lime trees was uprooted to allow the work to proceed, and although they have now been replaced it will take decades to re-establish their stature. The fine lime tree margin which formerly lined Tay Street gave Perth an affinity with Berlin, whose main city street, *Unter den Linden*, is named after its mile-long double avenue of lime trees.

High Street, Perth

No city worth its salt in the Edwardian years was complete without a tram service, and Perth Corporation indulged in this municipal extravagance, which seemed like a good idea at the time. Motor cars were in evidence – just – when this atmospheric scene was recorded. Surprisingly few of the buildings on the left (south) side of the street remain, one notable exception being the distinctive turreted building on the corner of the old Meal Vennel. The steeple of St Paul's Church – the second oldest church in the city – can be seen at the end of the street.

A 1906 scene with new tram number 3 forming almost the only item of traffic in George Street. The box on the right contains the section switches, as the tramway overhead power was supplied here (as can be seen from the overhead wires). A post office pillar-box now occupies the position of the old section box. Remarkably, most of the wall rosettes which supported the tramway overhead are still in place today, 70 years after the last tram passed. At the top of George Street, facing the Royal George Hotel, are old buildings beside the domed Marshall monument. These were removed in the 1930s for construction of the contiguous museum and art gallery. The Ionic columns fronting the Hay Marshall memorial building date from 1822 and are supposedly based on the Pantheon in Rome. Marshall Place, facing the South Inch at the other end of Tay Street, also commemorates Lord Provost Thomas Hay Marshall, one of Perth's many gifted benefactors. Credit is given to him for the planning of much of Georgian Perth.

An Edwardian postcard view of the High Street with tram 12 heading for the Cross. Sun shades are in evidence and there is an advertising cart on the right. The sender took his life in his hands by recording his message thus: 'Staying here for the night among the Unfair Maids of Perth – dirty weather'. The allusion is, of course to Sir Walter Scott's novel *The Fair Maid of Perth*. A modern bronze statue of a bench with seated figure of the maid, Catherine Glover, graces the east end of the pedestrianised part of the High Street.

A busy scene at South Methven Street from a card posted in January 1908. On the left are two wagonettes with top-hatted drivers carrying a wedding party from St Paul's Church, whose east windows face the street. The church was built in 1806–7 at a cost of £7,000. It could accommodate 1,000 worshippers in what was described in 1892 as 'an octagonal building of no architectural excellence, surmounted with a tall steeple'. A tram heading for the Cross disappears round the corner into the High Street, and on the right is a well-dressed lady cyclist. A note on the reverse of the card reads 'Little David is in the middle of this pc', and sure enough 'X' marks the spot where he is standing. The church has remained empty and unused for some years, but there is at the time of writing hope that new life might be breathed into the historic old building.

Trams ran along Kings Place on their route to Craigie terminus. Ninety or so years ago these fine Georgian villas facing the South Inch were town houses belonging to Perth's professional elite; now many are given over to office or guest house use. Car 10 was one of three trams built three inches lower than the others to give clearance below the old railway arch in King Street. The present girder bridge replaced the arch in 1907 and hence the need for special trams for this route was removed. Behind the tram is the crown steeple of St Leonard's-in-the-Fields Free Church, reminiscent of that of St Giles Cathedral in Edinburgh. While St Leonard's steeple dates only from 1885–6, that of St Giles goes back to the fifteenth century.

The end of the line at Craigie tram terminus at Priory Place. Car 11 was the second of the 'low three', which were originally painted green to differentiate and set them apart from the other nine cars, all of which were dark red. It is remarkable that despite provision of electricity for the use of the trams, street lighting is still by gas. The scene has changed little, but with gas lamps and tram overhead poles a thing of the past. Even then the presence of the tram terminus in the narrow street created a traffic hazard, so an extension of a few yards was constructed in 1910 to take the cars beyond the crossroads.

Infirmary and York Place, Perth

A 1906 postcard of York Place, Glasgow Road from the Caledonian Road junction. On the right is the classical facade of old county and city infirmary which dated from 1836. This became a Red Cross hospital during World War I, then a tuberculosis sanatorium. For many years afterwards it was headquarters for several departments of Perth County Council. It now fulfils its third incarnation as the A. K. Bell Library, opened by Charles, Prince of Wales in 1995. Tramcar 6 is en route from Cherrybank to Scone. The Waverley Hotel still occupies the corner site, while beyond are the twin spires of the church building now used by the Trinity Church of the Nazarene.

James Kelly, photographer, of 25 York Place, was obviously into publicity; but is he the driver or the Stan Laurel lookalike leaning on the radiator of what his advertising postcard described as 'Kelly's No 1 touring car' – a Daimler, registration ES 140. The leather box would be for the photographer's large glass negatives. This postcard, sent to Miss Taylor in Methven in July 1913, advises: 'I have your picture ready. You might call first time you are in'. Kelly gave up photography in 1926 and took up a second career as publican of the Empire Bar at 20 Princes Street.

CITY OF PERTH

CO-OPERATIVE SOCIETY LIMITED

SCOTT · STREET.

CITY OF PERTH CO-OPERATIVE SOCIETY LTD.

16 H.P. ALBION

Perth Co-operative Society had several different departments, and in 1911 purchased this 16 horsepower Albion lorry, ES 735, which had a detachable body. It was painted dark blue and lined and lettered in white. Note the acetylene lamps and the brass bulb horn. The co-operative movement was a national phenomenon and virtually every town and village had its co-op store. Many people depended on the co-op dividend to purchase small luxuries.

ES 1066 was a 1913 Lacre pantechnicon operated by Love's of St John's Place and South Street. Lanarkshire-born Thomas Love established a grocery business in Leonard Street in 1869 and later commenced regular household goods and furniture auctions on the site of the old Fleshmarket – now where the City Hall stands. The Canal Street furnishings building followed in 1906 and was at one time the coach-building yard of William Thomson. Canal Street was built over part of the old Town's Lade. Love's regular Friday auctions formed a major part of Perth's social scene. Lacre vehicles took their name from Long Acre in London where they were originally manufactured. The earliest Lacres were actually 'badge-engineered' Albions carrying the Lacre name.

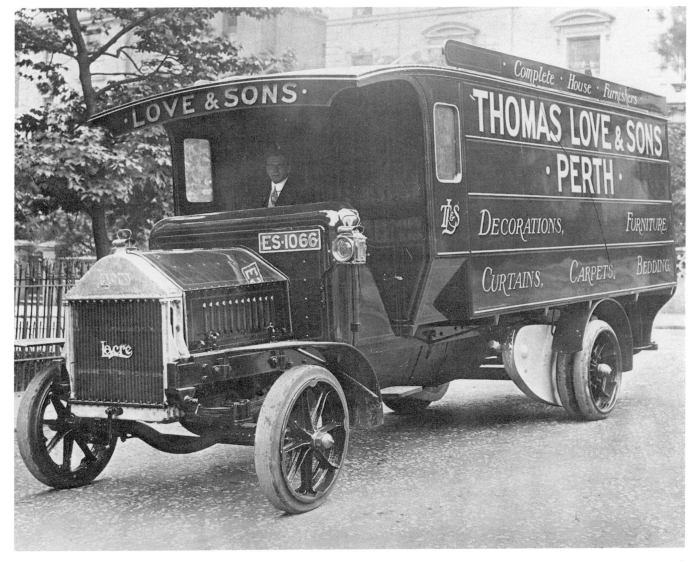

A charabanc outing in one of Valentine's vehicles *c*.1920. Based at Valentine's Buildings, 15 King Edward Street (since demolished), the company were agents for both Argyll and Austin cars. This charabanc may in fact be a Daimler, although Valentine purchased two Straker–Squire 32-seat charabancs in 1920. The photograph dates from after the incorporation of Valentine's Charabancs as a limited company. They only ran tours, excursions and private hire, never operating any stage services. W. Alexander of Falkirk acquired the charabanc touring side of the business in July 1935. Valentine's ceased trading in 1983.

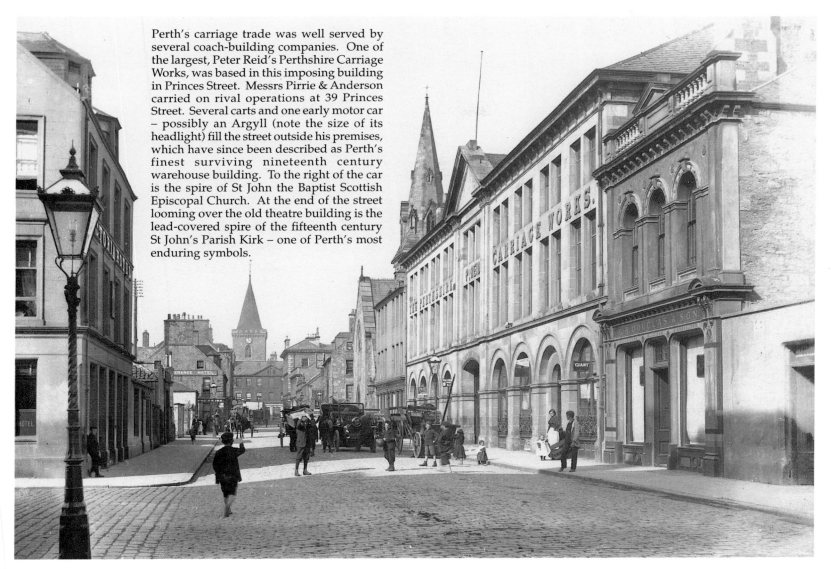

Perth's carriage trade was well served by several coach-building companies. One of the largest, Peter Reid's Perthshire Carriage Works, was based in this imposing building in Princes Street. Messrs Pirrie & Anderson carried on rival operations at 39 Princes Street. Several carts and one early motor car – possibly an Argyll (note the size of its headlight) fill the street outside his premises, which have since been described as Perth's finest surviving nineteenth century warehouse building. To the right of the car is the spire of St John the Baptist Scottish Episcopal Church. At the end of the street looming over the old theatre building is the lead-covered spire of the fifteenth century St John's Parish Kirk – one of Perth's most enduring symbols.

Perth's City Hall was newly built when this picture was taken *c*.1912. Designed with imposing Ionic columns in the grand civic style, it suited a confident city (no doubt it was never known as the Town Hall). Although the possibility of replacing it was explored in recent years when the fabric became poorly maintained, it now appears to have had a reprieve and should serve the inhabitants of the Fair City for many years to come. Note the horse cab to the right and the splendidly ornate decorative 'cherubs' at the corners of the building's roof line.

The City Hall was (and still is) the preferred venue for major events in Perth. The bazaar advertised here took place shortly after the First World War to raise money for St Paul's UF Church in New Row (not to be confused with St Paul's Church of Scotland at South Methven Street). An important fund-raiser, the young man in his best clothes wheels a barrow containing the message 'Pennies for Daddy's Bazaar Please'. The couple standing behind him are in all probability his parents, Revd and Mrs Charles Walls – but who is the Harry Lauder impersonator on the left? In 1920 St Paul's UF was taken back into the established church as St Columba's.

Perth Coronation Procession, 1911.
Car of Britannia.

A memorial procession was held on Coronation Day, 22 June 1911, to celebrate the crowning of King George V. Numerous decorated horse-drawn floats wound their way from the South Inch via South Street and the High Street to North Inch, and were apparently photographed from every vantage point judging by the many postcards of the scene which still survive. Here is the 'Car of Britannia', with onlookers crowding the windows of McIntyre & Stewart's tearoom at the corner of St John Street. Miss Morna Macgregor took the part of Britannia on her 'ship', attended by twelve boy sailors who walked behind her and were followed by 'cars' representing England, Scotland, Perth, Ireland, Wales, Canada, Australia, New Zealand, South Africa, India, and finally one for the remaining Crown Colonies. Considerable local disquiet was expressed that the English car should precede that of Scotland. Perth was awash with Coronation celebrations, and all trams in service were decorated.

As a major route centre, Perth was a rail junction of great importance. The first railway to reach the city – albeit only as far as Barnhill – was the Dundee & Perth (later part of the Caledonian) in 1847. The General Railway Station (so-called to distinguish it from a second small station at Princes Street) was reconstructed and enlarged in 1865 and 1885–1886, then remodelled again with significantly fewer track facilities in the 1970s. Here two of the Caledonian Railway's immaculately polished blue locomotives wait to start south to Carlisle on the 12.15 p.m. express in the halcyon days of rail transport prior to World War One.

The north end of the long through platform was the Highland Railway's domain. In this picture, according to the station clock, there are only two minutes to wait before the 11.50 service to Inverness sets off on its 114 mile journey. Mail trains did the journey in just over three hours, but some intrepid travellers had to survive a five hour test of endurance. The locomotive is no. 144, which was built in 1900 and named *Blair Castle* after Blair Atholl Castle, seat of the Duke of Atholl, a director of the company. Note the wooden steps which were kept handy for passenger use in case a train was longer than the platform.

There was a platform north of the Glasgow Road bridge where trains stopped while tickets were checked. 'Strath' class locomotive no. 91, *Strathspey*, heads this Highland Railway train. To the east of the line are the large goods and cattle transfer yards that served the nearby markets. The chimney of Pullar's of Perth dyeworks can be seen, and at the left-hand edge of the picture the road bridge taking Long Causeway over the railway. The site of the freight yards has now been given over to a commercial and shopping complex.

The third main railway to use Perth General Station was the North British, which operated trains to Edinburgh by way of Glenfarg and the Forth Bridge; to Dundee via St Fort; and to Ladybank in Fife. The Edinburgh expresses usually included through carriages from Inverness brought down by the Highland line. The locomotive pictured here is 'Atlantic' type no. 510, named *The Lord Provost* – the last of this type supplied to the company. It had a life of only 15 years. One hour was allowed for the 47½ mile trip from Perth to Edinburgh.

Flooding of parts of Perth has long been a fairly regular feature of life in the city. The ticket platform, seen in the picture on page 27, is the location for this First World War vintage view. It was taken on 8 July 1916 looking north from Glasgow Road, with the locomotive shed of the Highland Railway to the left.

FLOOD AT PERTH STATION 8716

An Edwardian scene showing the outside of Perth General Station from Leonard Street, with Cross Street leading off to the left. Facing the camera is the entrance for the Dundee platforms. These station buildings dated from the 1885–1886 reconstruction, and their appearance has not been improved by the recent addition of a modern Scotrail booking office. The lady is suitably dressed for cycling in her ankle-length skirt. The Royal British Hotel (left) – now Royal British House – has lost its contiguous tenement and bar, and the space is used as a car park for the Queen's Hotel next door.

29

In the 1930s the London, Midland & Scottish Railway (which was formed in 1923 and included the Highland and Caledonian Railways) experimented with 'Sentinel' steam railcars in an attempt to reduce costs on branch lines with limited traffic potential. One of these 'chip-cairts', as they were sometimes called, sits at the short bay platform at the north end of Perth station where it will form the afternoon train for Methven, calling at Ruthven Road, Almondbank and Tibbermore on its 7½ mile journey. Between 25 and 30 minutes were allowed for this journey, which can be accomplished comfortably today by car in just over 10 minutes – obeying all the speed limits. Methven lost its rail service in September 1937, perhaps not surprisingly.

Perthshire is not an industrial county, but bleaching and dyeing were exceptions, benefiting from the abundance of clean, pure water. At one time it took up to twelve weeks to bleach linen and cotton, but improved methods reduced this to three weeks. Over 200 people were employed at the bleachworks at Luncarty in the middle of the nineteenth century. To provide power some works produced their own electricity, but others used considerable volumes of coal and, in consequence, owned their own wagons to ensure priority of supply. The date of construction, 1899, can be discerned on this piece of local transport history, a curiosity now, but then an essential cog in the manufacturing process.

A busy scene at South Street Port, probably dating from the early 1920s. Heading west along County Place is a fine bull-nose Morris with its soft top folded back on this day of sunshine and strong shadows. The busy tram en route to Scone turns left into South Methven Street. On the right the 'wheels' theme is embodied in the bicycle and the street sweeper's barrow. Crossing over part of South Street is an open-sided delivery lorry.

North Inch, one of the city's several green 'lungs', forms a fitting foreground to this 1920s picture of Smeaton's bridge. Note the tram; these finally disappeared from the streets of Perth in February 1929 after severe competition from buses. No doubt when the photograph was taken the perambulator was the latest style. This Inch (from the Gaelic for 'small island') was the scene in 1396 of the Battle of the Clans, fought between the chosen representatives of the Kays and Chattons. Thirty from each side took arms to resolve a long-standing feud. Such was the spectacle that King Robert III came to view it!

The South Inch occupies a similar riverside location to its northerly partner, but is separated from the river by Shore Road, leading to the harbour. During the last major flood in 1993 this area was under over two feet of water. The north-east corner has long been the established venue for the 'shows', and is still regularly used for this purpose. In this Edwardian scene – with the elegant and distinctive waterworks chimney in the background – the jungle ride and swing chairs are in evidence, along with the swing boats to the left.

Show Ground, South Inch, Perth. T.S.P.

The North Inch, Perth.

The large, flat area on the North Inch formed an ideal cricket ground. Cricket is not often associated with Scotland, but Perthshire Cricket Club has played here, on what is possibly the oldest wicket in Scotland, as far back as 1826–1827. In one nineteenth century match Perth took on Scotland – and won! The wicket has also been the venue for Scottish international test matches. This particular game has attracted a large crowd – the mobile members of which have deposited their cycles on the turf. Perhaps the green sward benefited from its not infrequent inundations from the River Tay, although the new £25 million flood defence scheme should ensure that such events are now a thing of the past.

On the left of this view of Tay Street is the pillar guarding the west end of the Victoria Bridge. To the right is the Grecian portico of the old Perthshire County Council buildings, now occupied by the Sheriff Court. The original columns were made to be incorporated into a reconstructed facade for Broomhall House in Fife, but the Broomhall stone was rejected after construction, then replaced by Craigleith sandstone from near Edinburgh. Also to be seen is the original 1881 museum building belonging to the Perthshire Society of Natural Science, which moved to extended premises at the top of George Street in 1935. A variety of wheels complement the scene – from the motorcycle and sidecar heading north on the otherwise deserted street – to the ice-cream cart and the child's pushchair on the left. The new flood prevention walls have altered the vista along the whole length of Tay Street.

Tay Street, Perth

Here the photographer has turned 180 degrees to look north along Tay Street. The other pier at the end of the Victoria Bridge is on the right, with the old bridge in the distance behind it. The street is remarkably quiet when contrasted with today's hectic scene at this busy traffic light-controlled intersection. In the 1920s and 30s, Tay Street was much used as a bus and charabanc stance, and several such vehicles stand below the lime trees in the distance across from the end of the High Street. Note the pony cart in centre stage and the elegant baby carriage on the left, the focus of much female attention.

Itinerant photographers often photographed buses and their crews at termini, hoping for at least two sales, and here Perth's Tay Street has proved to be a fertile hunting ground. This little Commer, seen with proud driver and comely conductress, was operated by Stanley Fuller of Newburgh. Fuller ran a motley collection of vehicles which included such unusual makes as Berliet, Cottin et Desgouttes, and the American Chevrolet and United marques. His business was purchased in November 1927 by the Wemyss Tramway Company of Fife and amalgamated with their associated General Motor Carrying Company based in Kirkcaldy.

In addition to the multitude of private operators, Perth Corporation ran its own small bus fleet, originally as an adjunct to the tram service and latterly as its replacement. This fine view shows a 32-seat Thornycroft UB, registration number GS 368, which was purchased in 1928 with bodywork by Ransome Sims and Jeffries of Ipswich. Numbered 4 by Perth Corporation, it passed to W. Alexander Ltd. of Falkirk when they acquired the Corporation Transport Department on 16 May 1934. The destination is Rose Crescent but the significance of the letter T above is unknown. The distinctive coat of arms carried by the Transport Department buses was in evidence until the 1970s on Corporation refuse wagons!

Well-remembered local baker William Adie, who had shops in Atholl Street, Melville Street and South Methven Street, bought his Austin 7 van, GS 1278, in 1929. Perhaps a Perth resident with a long memory can advise if this is Mr Adie himself or one of his sons. It is not certain where the photograph was taken, but we can be fairly sure that the fine decorative cast iron railings in front of the buildings would have been cut down for 'salvage' during the first year of the Second World War. It is said that very little of the scrap thus generated ever saw any beneficial use for the war effort.

In the 1930s some famous locomotives were to be seen on the Perth to Dundee trains. Masquerading as plain LMS no. 14752 is the renowned Caledonian 4-6-0 – formerly no. 903, *Cardean*, and the pride of the line. She is seen here at the east end of platform 2 on 16 August 1930, awaiting the 'right – away' for the twenty mile run to 'Juteopolis'. Today 22 minutes are allowed for the journey, now to Tay Bridge Station, then to the old Dundee West Station. For this most trains – which did however make several stops – were allowed 55 minutes.

Perth was a Mecca for the railway enthusiast, and this particular shot was taken in March 1931 south of the General Station. Constructed to a design of the Great Central Railway, and used by the Railway Operating Department on the continent during the First World War, 2-8-0 no. 6544 eventually came into the ownership of the London & North Eastern Railway.

Towards the latter days of operation by steam locomotives, the class 5 LMS style was a frequent sight. Seen on 16 April 1962, no. 44978 is waiting at the south end of Perth General Station. It was photographed from the bridge at St Leonard's Bank, to which there was then a footbridge connection. This was a favourite vantage point for the railway photographer.

For several years in the twenties, the famous Caledonian Railway locomotive no. 123 had run passenger trains along the relatively level line to Dundee as LMS 14010. Fortunately its historic significance was appreciated, and it was preserved for future generations to admire – a beautiful example of Victorian locomotive engineering at its best. In June 1960 it returned to Perth, and is seen on the centre track between the two curved platforms used by trains to and from Dundee. Attracting admiring looks from bystanders, attention has to be drawn to the Scottish thistles on – and below – the buffers. In the halcyon days of steam, when a crew was always allocated to the same locomotive, they frequently decorated the smokebox with masonic or patriotic symbols. Of course only a colour photograph could do justice to the striking Caledonian blue livery. The diesel sat alongside pales to insignificance by comparison. Today the locomotive can still be viewed, but only as a static exhibit, in the Museum of Transport at Glasgow's Kelvin Hall.

Jeanfield, Perth.

In 1908 Jeanfield Road had been proposed as a route for tramway construction by Perth Corporation, but despite being granted the necessary Parliamentary Act the plans were never implemented (perhaps in retrospect the ratepayers were better off without the expense). The Goodlyburn residents had petitioned for the line, but had to wait until the 1920s for a transport link, when the Corporation eventually – and a trifle reluctantly – introduced a bus service. Today the gas lamps have gone, and it would be difficult to find a time of day when just one motor vehicle was to be seen. The stepped red sandstone terrace of West Grove Avenue now faces, across the street, Perth Royal Infirmary.

It seems like yesterday, but in fact this scene is over 60 years old, dating from the summer of 1939. A points policeman controls traffic on the High Street and Kinnoul Street/Scott Street junction and horse-drawn traffic is still in evidence (sometimes the 'evidence' was keenly sought and used by gardeners in their rose beds). While the streetscape appears little changed, in fact there is little that has not changed. Many of the nineteenth century frontages have been replaced by – in some cases unutterably dull – twentieth century architecture. The post office building on the right was probably too large for its location – but has

its replacement added to the elegance of this focal point of the centre of the city? Greater freedom of movement has followed the giving over of the street to pedestrians. Perth is most fortunate that, unlike many economic centres, it has been able to retain many small local shops in the centre. While the multiple stores are present, they have not swamped local enterprise, and Perth remains a vibrant community shopping centre.

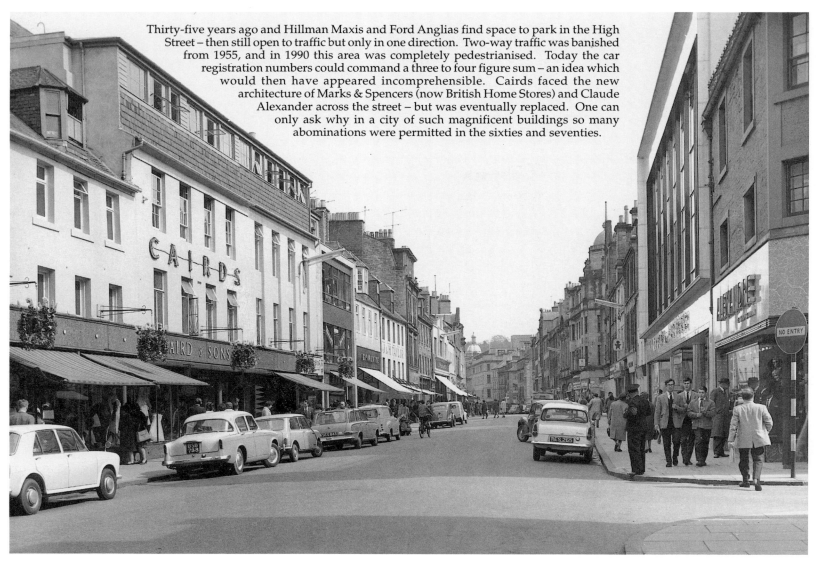

Thirty-five years ago and Hillman Maxis and Ford Anglias find space to park in the High Street – then still open to traffic but only in one direction. Two-way traffic was banished from 1955, and in 1990 this area was completely pedestrianised. Today the car registration numbers could command a three to four figure sum – an idea which would then have appeared incomprehensible. Cairds faced the new architecture of Marks & Spencers (now British Home Stores) and Claude Alexander across the street – but was eventually replaced. One can only ask why in a city of such magnificent buildings so many abominations were permitted in the sixties and seventies.

King Edward Street in the same era as the picture opposite with the Edward VII memorial cross surrounded by the short-lived 1960s St John's Square low-rise shopping area. The St John's Centre which replaced it opened in 1987. King Edward Street itself was a creation of the early years of last century when a dilapidated series of old wynds was cleared and the area 'improved'. (At one time it was proposed as the location for a central tram depot to avoid the 'dead' mileage of all trams having to return each night to Scone – would the locals have considered that as an improvement?) Wallaces department store at the High Street junction was pulled down in 1980, and the site is now occupied by a branch of Frasers. A Hillman Minx represents the British motor industry, but other cars to the fore are a Volkswagen Beetle, a Renault and a German-registered Mercedes. The cross structure is a close copy of Edinburgh's.

The fine flowing lines of the Queen's Bridge, recorded just a year after construction in this 1961 picture. The volume of traffic carried has increased remarkably over the years. This almost sylvan scene shows the graceful bridge well framed by the lime tree avenue. To the right is the older (but not the first) railway bridge from Barnhill on the line to Dundee. Newly built flood defence walls have replaced the railings and lifebelt. The two-kilometre honey-coloured sandstone wall incorporates ten very attractive small stone sculptures by Gillian Forbes which add considerably to the aesthetic satisfaction of the 'barrier' presented by the stone – but it must be a cause of concern to note the rapidity with which some areas of stone are being colonised by an unattractive green algae growth.

When this photograph was taken in 1950, the local buses had their own distinctive dark red livery to differentiate them from the rest of the Alexander fleet. Cherrybank to Scone remained the main route, just as it had been when the horse – then electric – trams had been running. The poles on the right, carrying the street lighting, were those erected in 1905 to hold the tramway overhead electric wires, and had ornamental cast iron bases each carrying the Perth coat of arms. The former Scone tram depot, just to the photographer's right, retained its tramway track in the yard until relatively recently.

For many years Murray Street was the location for Alexander's bus office in the city – note the window poster with its admonition to 'See Bonnie Scotland by Bluebird' – which was a much more likely way to spend one's holidays in the 1950s than sun-seeking on the 'Costas'. The queue is unlikely to be for the Auchterarder bus, and more probably for the Playhouse cinema next door. The 1933 cinema's Art Deco frontage is still worth seeing. It is said that the building was erected in only nine weeks – a feat which would be difficult to emulate even today.